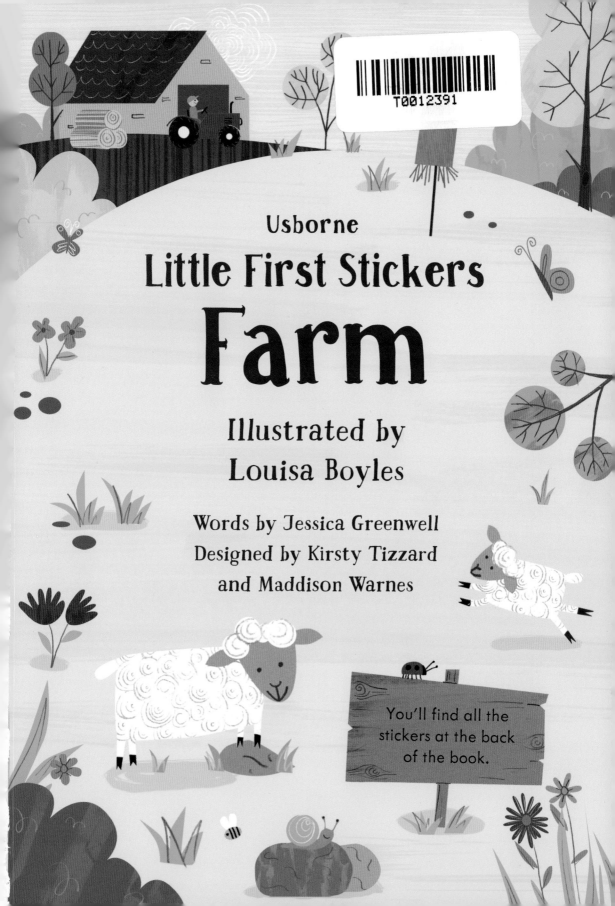

Usborne
Little First Stickers
Farm

Illustrated by
Louisa Boyles

Words by Jessica Greenwell
Designed by Kirsty Tizzard
and Maddison Warnes

You'll find all the stickers at the back of the book.

In the farmyard

The farmyard is a busy place. Can you add all the people, animals, tractors and trucks to this picture?

Find a place to park the tractor.

Stick some horses
in the stables.

Add a gate and the
farm name here.

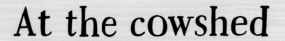

At the cowshed

The cows wake up early with the sun and
a noisy cockerel calls, 'cock-a-doodle-dooo!'.

Fill the picture with
cows and calves.

Stick on the farmer feeding
some hungry cows.

Stick some cows in the cowshed.

Lots of sheep

The sheep and the lambs in the meadow graze on the grass and snooze in the sunshine.

Add some more sheep to the picture.

Find a friendly sheepdog to look after the sheep.

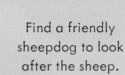

At the pigsty

Pigs love muddy puddles. The piglets are very playful, all splashing and snorting noisily.

Find a spot for some pigs eating from their trough.

Stick some playful piglets in the mud.

At the pond

The farm's pond is home to lots of animals and insects. Can you add them all to the picture?

Stick on a frog
hopping off this rock.

Fill the pond with
ducks and ducklings.

Hens and chicks

Hens lay eggs inside the henhouse, and
the farmer collects them every day.
Stick on all the hens, chicks and eggs.

Find a place for a
basket of eggs.

How many chicks
can you find to add
to the picture?

Farm machines

There are lots of different machines on the farm, from trucks and tractors to combine harvesters. They all have different jobs to do. Stick them on the road and in the fields.

Find a trailer to add to the back of this tractor.

Find a windmill to add to the picture.

What could you stick on the road?

The vegetable patch

The vegetables growing here are almost ready to be picked.
Stick some more in the rows and add some tools, too.

Stick on some
more rabbits.

Peas

Carrots

Add some
more signs to label
the vegetables.

Farm shop

This shop sells some of the things made on the farm.
Fill the shelves with things for sale, from fresh fruits
and vegetables to delicious cheese.

Tasters

Put some milk, cheese
and cream in here.

Eggs

Country show

Every year farmers bring their best animals and crops to this country show. There are competitions to enter and prizes to be won.

Which animal could be stepping out of this trailer?

Put some more stalls inside the food tent.

Give each horse a rosette. Who will you give 1st place to?

Meet the animals

This is where children can feed and stroke the animals. Add them all to the picture and see which animal you like the best.

Stick on some children holding animals.

Put some fluffy rabbits in here.

In the farmyard pages 2-3

Dog

Mini tractor

Tractor

Cat

Beehives

Geese

Cart

Wheelbarrows

Horses

Farm truck

Littlebrook Farm

Gate

Cows

Farmer

Goslings

Geese

Calves

Lots of sheep page 6

Nest

Sheep

Lambs

Sheepdog

At the pigsty page 7

Pigs

Piglets

At the pond page 8

Frogs

Lily pad

Ducks and ducklings

Goose

Hens and chicks page 9

Chicks

Egg basket

Hen and feeder

Farm machines pages 10–11

Hay bales

Apple trees

Windmill

Scarecrows

Baler

Cyclist

Horse riders

Tractors

Farm truck

MILK

Milk tanker

Trailer

Crops

The vegetable patch page 12

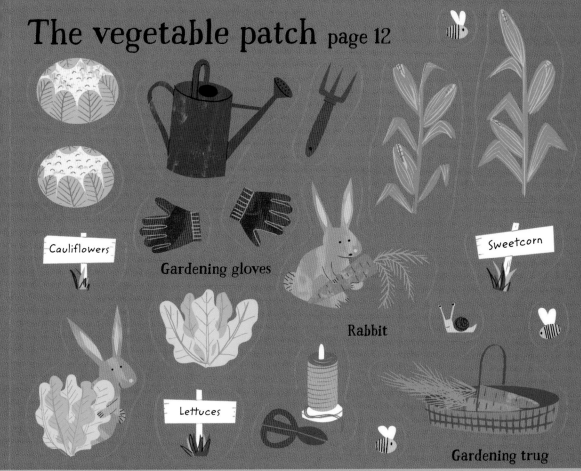

Cauliflowers

Gardening gloves

Rabbit

Sweetcorn

Lettuces

Gardening trug

Farm shop page 13

Potatoes

Carrots

Garlic

Honey

Fruit jams

Milk

Cheese

Cream

Apples

Country show pages 14–15

Cake stall

Prize vegetables

2nd

1st

Main arena

Food tent

Gloucester Old
Spot pig

1st

Dogs

Highland bull

1st

Food
tent

Alpaca

1st

2nd

3rd

Rosettes

Wensleydale sheep

3rd

3rd

1st

2nd

Meet the animals page 16

Shetland pony

Ducks

Food

Lamb

Rabbits

Baby goats

Guinea pigs

You can use these stickers anywhere in the book.